All You Wanted To Know About

Baby Names for the New Millennium

Editorial Board

Madhvi Kapur
Neeta Datta
Sharmistha Dash

New Dawn

NEW DAWN
a division of Sterling Publishers (P) Ltd.
A-59, Okhla Industrial Area, Phase-II, New Delhi-110020.
Tel: 26387070, 26386209; Fax: 91-11-26383788
E-mail: info@sterlingpublishers.com
www.sterlingpublishers.com

All You Wanted to Know about Baby Names:
For the New Millennium
© 1999, Sterling Publishers Private Limited
ISBN 81 207 2270 1
Reprint 2001, 2005, 2007

All rights are reserved. No part of this publication may be reproduced, stored in a retrieval system or transmitted, in any form or by any means, mechanical, photocopying, recording or otherwise, without prior written permission of the publisher.

Published by Sterling Publishers Pvt. Ltd., New Delhi-110020.
Lasertypeset by Vikas Compographics, New Delhi-110020.
Printed at Sterling Publishers Pvt. Ltd., New Delhi

Contents

Preface	5
1. Things to consider when naming your baby	7
2. Birthstones and Flowers	9
3. Boys	11
4. Girls	92

Every baby born into the world is a finer one than the last.

Charles Dickens

Preface

Everyone has a name. A name gives a person an identity. In most countries, people have at least two names, a name that a child has been given, and a family name. The family name is also called a surname or last name which is common to all family members. The surname is derived either from the village or tribe the family belongs to or from the kind of work they do for a livelihood.

The given name is the one that distinguishes the child from other family members. The given name and the family name together make up a person's legal name.

In southern India, people write their names differently. They have a house name which they add before their own name. They also use their father's name before their own name. For example if a family name is Thykadavil, and the father's name is George, and the given name is Abraham then the person's name is Thykadavil George Abraham (the first name is the house name, the second, the father's name and the last, the person's name). The house name and the father's name are written as initials. So the person's name will be written as T.G. Abraham.

A girl child is usually named after birds, flowers, deities or the softer qualities of a woman. A boy child is usually named after qualities of valour, honour, bravery, or joy.

With the arrival of a new born, the parents are faced with the problem of naming a child. All parents wish to give their child a name which is meaningful and at the same time exclusive.

With this thought in mind and keeping in mind our culture and heritage, we set upon the task of compiling names which are not common.

Most of the names have more than one meaning. This comprehensive collection comprises names from religious texts, mythology, fables and literature.

THINGS TO CONSIDER WHEN NAMING YOUR BABY

Nationality	If parents select a foreign sounding name it should not be unpronounceable or unspellable.
Religion	Religion plays an important role in an Indian's life. Most of our names have some religious connotation, or belong to gods and goddesses.
Gender	In Sikh names, there is hardly any gender difference. The difference is apparent only when the suffix 'Singh' (for males) and 'Kaur' (for females) is added to the first name.
Number of Names	Many Indian communities follow the trend of adding the grandparents', parents' name before the child's name. The parents should give this a serious thought before burdening their child with a long name.
Pronunciation	Parents should choose a name that has a clear pronunciation.

Spelling	Many Indian names lend themselves to different spellings. The 'i' in a name is often replaced by 'ee'. For example, the name Nita can also be written as Neeta.
Uniqueness	Most parents today wish to give their child a unique name, a name which is very different. A child with an uncommon name feels good that he/she has a unique name. Many parents also combine names to give an unusual name to their child.
Initials	Before the parents finally settle for a name, they should also consider the child's initials. It can be embarrassing to have an initial like DAD or DUD.

So when naming your child, check out the initials that he/she will have as a result.

BIRTHSTONES AND FLOWERS

January
Birthstone : garnet
Flower : carnation

February
Birthstone : amethyst
Flower : violet

March
Birthstone : aquamarine
Flower : jonquil

April
Birthstone : diamond
Flower : sweet pea

May
Birthstone : emerald
Flower : lily of the valley

June
Birthstone : pearl
Flower : rose

July
Birthstone : ruby
Flower : lackspur

August
Birthstone : peridot
Flower : gladioli

September
Birthstone : sapphire
Flower : aster

October
Birthstone : opal
Flower : calendula

November
Birthstone : topaz
Flower : chrysanthemum

December
Birthstone : turquoise
Flower : narcissus

Aaddhar: foundation

Aahan: iron; sword

Abadhya: always victorious; unopposed

Abdar: glittering with water; wealthy

Abeesht: wanted, desired

Abhar: brilliant; magnificent; shining

Abhiveer: one who commands; one who is surrounded by heroes or warriors

Abrad: very cold; leopard

Abrak: the blessed one
Abyan: very clean
Abyaz: white
Abzar: powerful, mighty
Adavak: simple, uncomplicated
Adhiksit: king, lord
Adhish: lord, master
Adhit: scholarly, intelligent, wise
Adil: sincere
Adit: first
Adraksh: lightning
Adrij: belonging to the mountains
Advait: unique
Advik: unique
Advitiya: unique
Afrah: happiness
Afraz: height
Ahan: dawn, morning
Ahdas: new, novel
Ahim: warm, cloud; water; traveller

Akalank: without any flaws
Akhash: price, worth, value
Aksal: complete
Akshaj: diamond, lightning
Akshan: eye
Akshar: imperishable, forever
Akshath: unharmed
Aksheen: very strong
Akush: lap
Akyas: wise, intelligent
Alih: idol
Alya: apt
Amad: serious
Amal: pure, clean
Amitay: limitless
Amolik: priceless, precious
Anagh: sinless, pure, perfect
Ananjan: without any faults
Anantajit: always victorious
Anargh: priceless

Aniket: homeless; one who makes the world his home; a celestial being who was the king of the Anga dynasty

Animish: alert, vigilant; a god

Anirab: an angel who presides over fire

Aniran: eternal light

Anirvan: undying; god

Anish: foremost, important, supreme

Aniveshak: one who finds, seeker

Aniveshan: to find

Ansh: a part of something

Anuansh: generous, charitable

Anuranjan: name of a *raag*; love

Anuvind: one who receives; a cousin of Lord Krishna

Anuvrat: devoted, faithful

Aparaditya: enlightening; brilliant

Apratim: unequalled

Apurva: new; extrordinary; without comparison

Aranya: a forest; foreign land; desert

Archit: one who is worshipped, one who is honoured

Arenu: one who does not belong to earth, celestial

Arhant: non-violent, peaceful; worthy

Arhat: deserving

Arihan: one who kills enemies

Arjit: earned; acquired

Arkesh: sun

Armaan: wish, longing

Arnav: ocean

Arohan: to rise

Arsh: sky, space

Arshan: righteous

Arshya: righteous

Aruj: healthy

Aryaman: the sun; friend; son of Kasyapa and Aditi

Aryamik: noble, virtuous

Aryannam: nature-lover; forest dweller

Ashrey: shelter

Ashvant: follower of truth

Ayaan: nature, temperament

Ayuj: without a companion, without an equal

Badikh: important, prominent

Bahaj: jubilation, happiness, joy, rejoicing

Bahuvida: scholarly, wise, enlightened

Baladeya: giver of strength

Baladhika: unequalled in strength

Baladhya: full of strength

Balanuj: the younger brother of Balaram, another name for Krishna

Balaravi: the sun in the morning

Balark: the rising sun

Balarun: dawn

Balin: healthy; energetic; powerful

Banajita: one who conquers with arrows; another name for Vishnu

Basav: bull; mighty; masculine; a minister of a Jaina king who developed Vira-Saiva system

Bayaz: white, bright

Bhargava: radiant; related to Bhrigu, an archer; another name for Sukra regent of the planet Venus and preceptor of demons, Parasurama, Jamadagni, Markandeya and Shiva

Bhasvan: radiant; another name for Surya

Bhautik: material, physical; radiant; pearl; another name for Shiva

Bhavik: devout; well-meaning; virtuous; happy

Bhuman: comprising all that exists; the earth

Bhumanyu: one who is accepted by all; devotee of the earth; grandson of Dushyant

Bhumitra: friend of the earth; a ruler

Bhuranyu: worshipped by the world; fast; anxious; efficent; changeable; a name for Vishnu and the sun.

Biren: lord of warriors, great warriors

Brihant: destroyer of the powerful; massive; grand; a king who fought on the side of the Paṇḍavas

Bushur: good news

Chaitnya: consciousness; wisdom; soul; mind; spirit; founder of the four principles of Vaishinav sect; a reincarnation of Krishna

Chaitya: pertaining to the mind; indivdual soul; a stupa built in Jain or Buddhist places of worship

Chaityak: abode of consciousness; a place of worship; a mountain near Magadha which is worshipped

Chanakya: the son of Chanak; author of *Arthashastra*

Chandan: sandalwood; auspicious; dear to the gods; soothing

Chandavikram: a fierce fighter; a prince

Chandavir: very brave; a Buddhist deity

Chandnin: anointed with sandalwood; another name for Shiva

Chandraditya: name of a king

Chandrajit: one who conquers the moon, surpassing the moon

Chandrat: the moon's nectar; fair; handsome; peaceful; nectar-like; a physician of Ancient India

Chaturnik: four-faced; a name for Varuna

Chayank: another name for the moon

Chetan: conscious, alive; visible; illustrious, soul; mind; man

Chetas: wisdom; grandeur; soul; heart; mind

Chinmay: intelligent; the supreme spirit

Chirantan: eternal, old

Chitraksh: speckle-eyed; unusual eyes; beautiful eyes; one of the sons of Dhrithrastra; a serpent lord.

Chitrarath: the sun; name of a gandharva

Chitrish: king of Chitra; wonderful lord; another name for moon

Dadhikra: born from the Ocean of Milk; fast-moving; a divine horse who personifies the morning sun

Dadhyan: seller of milk, one who brings the milk; a hermit who was taught by Indra the art of preparing rice for offering to the gods

Daityahan: killer of demons; another name for Shiva

Daivya: heavenly; grand; a messenger of the demons

Daksayan: coming from Daksa

Daksh: expert, talented; fit; fire; gold

Daksi: son of Daksa; precious son; son of a perfect being

Daman: efficent; powerful; mighty; first; foot of mountain

Damati: one who subdues a conquerer

Damik: earth, land, field

Danah: intelligent, knowledgeable

Darsh: worth looking at; the day of the new moon personified as the son of Dhatr; another name for Krishna

Darshish: mighty, powerful

Darun: as hard as wood

Dayamit: kind, merciful

Deshak: one who directs; guide; king

Devakirti: with divine fame

Devanath: lord of the gods, another name for Shiva

Devansh: a part of God, a partial incarnation of the gods

Devavrat: the favourite food of the gods; a religious oath; follower of a religious path; a brahmin born as bamboo from which Krishna made his flute; another name for Bhisma.

Devesth: best among the gods

Devhish: gift; generosity, charity

Devraj: king of the gods; a king in the court of Yama; another name for Indra

Devya: divine power

Dharman: bearer of Dharma, one who supports Dharma; a son of Brihadraja and father of Krtanjaya

Dharmayu: one who dedicates his life for Dharma; a Puru king who was the son of Raudrasva and Misrakesi

Dhavit: white; washed, pure, clean

Dhimant: wise, intelligent; another name for Brihaspati

Dhitik: wise; thoughtful; a Buddhist patriachal saint

Dhrishit: courageous, fearless, heroic

Dhruv: fixed, immortal, perpetual; the polar star personified as the son of Uttanapada and Suniti and the grandson of Manu; a son of Vasudev and Rohini; a Kaurava warrior, another name for Brahma, Vishnu and Shiva

Dhvanya: suggested; meaning; a son of Lakshman

Dikshit: initated into a religious order

Divij: born of the sky, heaven born, divine, a god

Divijat: born of the sky, born of heaven

Durva: heavenly grass

Dvarik: door attendant; one of the eighteen attendants of Surya

Dyumnik: inspired; grand; mighty; a son of Vashisth

Dyutit: enlightened; clear; shining

Eashan: another name for Lord Shiva

Ecchit: wanted, desired

Edhas: sacred wood; joy; wood used for sacrificial fire

Edhit: grown, advanced, evolved

Ekachit: possessing one's mind; complete concentration; calm, reposed

Ekagr: complete concentration; poised, peaceful; stable; alert

Ekantin: devoted to one object; a name for the follower of Vishnu

Ekaraya: one ruler

Ekatan: alert; concentrated

Elash: shining, a horse of the sun; a sage extolled in *Rig Veda*; a sage whom Indra helped against Surya

Elesh: king

Emet: desire; aspiration

Entilak: marked; another name for moon

Erman: friend; God

Ettan: breath

Evayavan: swift; granting wishes; another name for Vishnu

Faghyar: intelligent, like a scholar

Faham: wise; considerate

Fahim: wise, learned; prudent, sagacious

Faishah: head, principal; place of origin of a river or torrent

Faizah: achieving, attaining, accomplishing; possessing

Faizan: charitable; bountiful; benefit

Fakah: gay, happy

Fakhar: pride, fame; jewellery; excellence; nobility

Fakht: moonlight; moonbeam

Falih: prosperous, successful

Faqid: one who knows law and divinity; intelligent, judicious, understanding

Faraj: happiness; ease, relief

Fardin: one who has triple strength; first month of the Parsi year when the sun is in Aries

Farhad: digger of mines; cutter of stones; celebrated stonecutter who dug a canal through a mountain for his beloved Shirin

Farhan: happiness, joyful, gay

Farhat: happiness, joy

Farid: solitary; different; unique; unequalled; exquisite

Farjat: happiness, freedom from sorrow

Farman: order, command; royal patent

Farmand: intelligent; pure

Fartash: existence

Farud: solitary; unique

Faruh: happiness, gay

Faruz: turquoise

Farwah: covering; a crow

Faryad: surprise; cry for help; complaint

Farzand: child; son

Fashan: mace of iron; silver or gold

Fastyar: commander of 1000 men

Fatiq: bright, shining; east; dawn

Fayyaz: generous, charitable; bountiful; merciful

Fazil: talented; scholar; another name for God

Firnas: powerful; brave; thick-necked lion

Firoh: happiness, joy

Firyal: adornment

Frado: first

Fragan: foundation, base, root

Fraron: honest, righteous

Frohar: angel, spirit, spirit which protects the soul as a guardian angel

Furozan: shining, bright, illuminated

Gadhij: son of Gadhi; another name for sage Visvamitra

Gadin: one who is armed with a club; another name for Krishna

Gajasya: elephant-faced, another name for Ganesha

Galav: to worship; a famous sage who was the son of Vishvamitra

Gambhir: deep, serious, thoughtful

Ganak: one who calculates, a mathematician, an astrologer; a collection of stars

Gandir: hero;

Gandiv: one who lights up the earth; conquerer of the earth; a magical bow which no weapon can damage; the famous bow of Arjuna made by Brahma which could fight 1,00,000 people at the same time

Ganin: one who has attendants

Gariman: ponderouness; one of the eight siddhis of Shiva

Garisth: heaviest, greatest, house of greatness; a sage who was a devotee of Indra and sat in his assembly; a demon

Garlesh: master of a cave

Gaurang: fair-complexioned; another name for Vishnu, Shiva, Krishna and sage Chaitnya

Gaurij: son of Parvati, another name for Kartikeya

Gaurish: lord of Gauri, a royal sage who was part of Yama's assembly; another name for Shiva and Varuna

Gavendra: bull; lord of oxen; another name for Vishnu

Gavisth: the house of light; the sun as the giver of light

Gayan: the sky

Gayand: an elephant

Girik: the heart of god; an attendant of Shiva,

Girikshit: one who resides on the mountain; another name for Shiva

Giriman: mountain-like, a mighty elephant

Girindra: lord of the mountains; the highest mountain; another name for Shiva

Girith: wise; another name for Brihaspati

Grahin: related to the planets

Grahish: lord of the planets, another name for the sun and Saturn

Grihit: comprehended; accepted

Gurdeep: light of guru

Gurudyal: a kind teacher

Gurupriya: a dear student

Habib: beloved

Hafiz: protected

Hakesh: lord of sound

Haleen: mild

Hameed: a friend

Hansaj: son of a swan

Hanumesh: lord of Hanuman, another name for Rama

Haradik: the king and soul of love; another name for Brahma, the sun; and Vishnu; a kshatriya king.

Hardirk: honesty; heartfelt

Harendra: Indra and Shiva together

Hareshit: cheerful, gay

Hariaksh: the pivot of Vishnu, the eye of Vishnu; the eye of the lion, another name for the lion, Kubera and Shiva

Hariank: in the lap of Vishnu; a king of the Anga dynasty; father of king Brihadratha

Hariashv: the horse of Vishnu; one of 5000 sons born to Daksha and Asikini; a king of the solar dynasty of Ayodhya who married Madhavi, the daughter of Yayati; the father of king Sudeva of Kasi

Haridr: the yellow colour, turmeric; a god

Harij: the horizon

Harikesh: one with yellow hair; one of the seven main rays of the sun; a yaksa; a son of Syamaka; another name for Vishnu, Shiva

Harin: deer; sun; wheatish-complexioned

Harinaksh: one with eyes like a deer; another name for Shiva

Harinank: spotted like the deer; camphor; another name for Chandra

Harinesh: the lord of deer; lion

Harit: greenery; a gentle breeze; a son of Vishwamitra

Harsh: happy, joy; one of the three sons of Dharma; king Harshvardhan of north India; a son of Krishna

Harshad: very happy

Harshak: happy, cheerful; a son of Chitragupt

Harshal: happy; a lover

Harshan: causing happiness; one of the five arrows of Kama

Haryaksh: lion, the zodiac sign of Leo; a son of Prithu; another name for Kubera and Shiva

Haryshv: a solar dynasty king of Ayodhya; another name for Indra, Shiva

Haseen: handsome

Hassan: a saint

Hatakesh: lord of gold; another name for Shiva

Hatish: one who has no wishes

Hemadri: golden mountain; another name for mountain Sumeru

Heman: the colour golden yellow, made of gold; the jasmine blossom; saffron flower; another name for the planet Mercury

Hemant: the winter season

Hemanya: golden-bodied

Himadri: peak of snow, the Himalayas

Hirang: diamond; as strong as a diamond; the thunderbolt of Indra

Hiranya: gold; very valuable; another name for Vishnu

Hiranyav: an ornament made of gold; belonging to God

Hiranyin: of gold

Hiren: lord of gems; very beautiful pearls

Hitashi: a well-wisher

Hridaya: heart

Hridayesh: lord of the heart

Hriman: one who removes sorrows; wealthy

Hussain: devout; grandson of Prophet Muhammad

Ibhya: one who has many attendants

Icchak: one who grants wishes; the citron tree

Iddham: bright; radiant; sunshine; light; heat

Idhant: bright, resplendent; pure, beautiful; sharp; a sage

Inan: the sun; ruler; lord and master

Inas: talented; mighty, bold; famous; another name for Surya

Inayat: benevolence

Indraj: born of Indra; another name for Valin

Indranuj: younger brother of Indra; another name for Vishnu

Indrejya: teacher of Indra; a good teacher; another name for Brihaspati

Indrink: as wished by Indra

Indris: lord

Inesh: a brave king; another name for Vishnu

Ingid: one who gives knowledge; a plant used in magical rites to ensure destruction of enemies

Inoday: sunrise

Intazar: hope

Iraish: lord of the earth; another name for Varuna, Vishnu and Ganesha

Iraj: born of the wind; another name for Hanuman, the son of the wind god, Vayu

Iravan: possessing water or milk; ocean; cloud; king; the son of Arjuna and Ulupi

Iresh: lord of the earth; another name for Vishnu, Varuna and Ganesha

Irith: belonging to the wind; perfume

Irm: like the wind; always moving; another name for Surya

Irmand: one who enjoys drinking; a flash of lighting; another name for Agni

Irshad: sign

Ishaan: bestowing wealth

Ishanam: light; grandeur

Ishat: excellence; greatness

Ishayu: fresh; mighty; courageous

Ishik: wanted; the silkcotton tree

Ishir: mighty; efficient; active; rejuvenating; another name for Agni

Ishit: longed for, wished for

Ishmin: efficient, fast; impulsive; wind-like

Ishrit: owner; lord of the universe

Ishya: the spring season

Istik: a brick used in preparing the ceremonial altar

Itish: a lord

Jaganant: one to whom the world belongs

Jagesh: lord of the world, another name for Vishnu

Jagish: lord of the world

Jagrani: alert; shining; another name for Agni and the sun

Jaijan: victory

Jaikrit: causing victory

Jaiman: victorious

Jairaj: a victorious ruler

Jairam: victorious Rama

Jaishnav: one who wishes for victory

Jaivant: long-lived

Jaivatrik: long-lived; one for whom long life is desired; son; another name for moon

Jalaj: born of water, the lotus; conchshell; another name for the moon

Jalaneel: the blue colour of the sea

Jalit: radiance; influence

Jameel: good-looking

Janav: one who protects men

Janesh: lord of men

Janisth: wanted by people

Janit: born

Jasamit: illustrious

Jatin: wearing twisted hair; an ascetic; another name for Shiva

Javas: efficient

Jayada: one leading to victory

Jayant: one who is victorious in the end; the moon

Jayesh: name of Bhima during the hiding period
Jayin: conqueror
Jenya: truth
Jivant: long-lived

Kaditul: a sword

Kairav: born of water; the white lotus

Kakand: gold

Kakkul: Bakula tree; a Buddhist monk

Kakshak: forest-dweller; a serpent born in the family of Vasuki

Kaksheyu: kept in the armpit; conquered; embarassed

Kalil: something which cannot be pierced; deep

Kalkrit: decided by time; constant; peacock; another name for the supreme spirit and the sun

Kalpesh: lord of perfection

Kalpit: conceived; apt, proper

Kaltr: a royal citadel; the seventh lunar mansion

Kalvik: sparrow

Kamaj: born of love; son of Kama; another name for Shiva and Karttikeya

Kaman: wished for, longed for; beautiful; another name for Kama and Brahma

Kamat: one who follows one's desires; unchecked; a king of Kamboj and member of the court of Yudhisthira; a serpent born in Dhritarastra's family

Kamayak: longed for; name of a forest

Kamayush: one who lives as long as he wants; another name for Garuda

Kamesth: desired by Kama; mango tree

Kamik: longed for, wished for

Kanav: able; expert; appreciated; honoured; wise; a sage of Kashyap family

Kanisth: the youngest

Kanvaka: son of a talented person

Kapiley: one who is brown coloured; a son of Vishvamitra

Karanj: born of hand; one who is obtained with difficulty; valuable

Karin: achieving; appreciate; pleasing

Karmanya: one who is good at his work, talented; hard-working

Kartik: one who gives courage and happiness; one who belongs to the month of *Kartik*

Kasayin: one who wears saffron clothes; a sage, a Buddhist monk

Kathit: well-said; one who is talked about and appreciated by all

Kautilya: author of the famous work called *Arthshastra* and an advisor to King Chandragupta

Kavindra: a prince among poets

Kavish: lord of poets; a good physician; a sage; another name for Shukra

Kavitv: wise; one who has talent for writing poetry

Ketan: house; flag, symbol

Khagesh: lord of birds, another name for Garuda

Khajit: one who conquers heaven; a Buddha

Khalin: a name for Mahavishnu and Shiva

Khashaya: air-borne

Kinjat: a blossom

Kirat: one who lives in caves; hunters belonging to a mountain tribe; Shiva in his form as a warrior of the Kirat tribe

Kirik: shining, bright

Kirin: one who appreciates; a poet, an author, a speaker

Kirit: a crown, crest, tiara

Kiritin: one who wears a crown; another name for Arjun and Indra

Kirti: illustrious

Krimish: lord of serpents

Kritagya: grateful

Kritak: unnatural; adopted; a son of Vasudev

Kritayush: one who lives as long as one wishes to, one who masters age

Kritharth: one who owns chariots

Krithasv: one who owns many horses, a good rider

Kshitij: son of the earth; a tree; the horizon

Ksitish: lord of the earth

Kunjit: hidden in the forest

Kuntesh: master of Kunti, another name of Pandu

Kushaksh: sharp-eyed

Kushalin: intelligent; auspicious; healthy

Kuvam: producer of the earth; another name for the sun

Laghat: the wind

Laksh: objective, aim, target

Lakshan: one with an auspicious mark

Lakshang: one with auspicious marks; one who achieves one's aim, successful

Lakshin: with an auspicious mark

Laksmanya: son of Lakshman; visible; far and wide; another name for Dhvanya

Lalitya: affectionate; good-looking

Lamak: a lover; a chivalrous man

Lashit: longed for, desired

Lauhit: made of metal; red; the trident of Shiva

Lavam: clove; tiny

Lavan: good-looking, beautiful; salty

Lavanik: good-looking, beautiful; salty

Lavanish: lord of the sea, another name for Varuna

Lavitr: the delicate one; another name for Shiva

Likhit: written; name of a sage

Madhuj: made of honey, sugar

Madhul: sweet; an intoxicating drink

Madhup: sweet; a bee

Madhurya: sweet, affectionate, charming

Madraj: son of Madra; another name for Salya

Madur: a bird

Madvan: intoxicating; delightful; another name for Shiva

Mahaj: born in a noble family

Mahaksh: large-eyed; another name for Shiva

Mahart: honest

Mahayya: one who is happy

Mahip: protector of the earth, a king

Mahir: talented, expert

Mahit: famous, illustrious; a river

Mahiyu: joyful, delighted

Mahtab: moon, moonlight

Mahya: one who is honoured; a tribe

Majeed: worshippable

Malhar: bringer of rains; a *raag* in Hindustani music related to the monsoon

Manaj: born of mind; another name for Kama

Manal: a bird, the Himalayan Monal Pheasant

Manan: meditation, thought; wisdom, comprehension

Manas: wisdom, understanding

Manav: a young boy; a pearl ornament of sixteen strings; one of the nine treasures of the Jainas

Mandit: decorated

Mandtish: most enjoyable

Manhan: a gift

Manhayu: generous

Manhisth: one who grants wishes, grants generously

Manik: a jewel

Manikya: ruby

Maninder: the chief of jewels, diamond

Manishin: thoughtful, wise

Manit: comprehended, understood; respected

Manivak: one who speaks beautifully; son of Bhavya and grandson of Priyavrata

Marank: marked by love

Marmit: the destroyer of Kama; another name for Shiva

Mayan: one who has no love for wealth

Mayank: spotted like the deer; another name for the moon

Mayas: happiness, joy

Medhas: sacrifice; a sage

Medhir: intelligent

Mehul: rain

Midhush: abundance; a son of Indra and Paulomi

Mihir: the sun

Mitul: in proper quantities, moderate

Mrigank: spotted like the deer; the moon; wind; camphor

Mudit: happy, gay, joyous

Mukul: bud

Nabhas: sky, mist, clouds, vapour; a month in the monsoon season

Nabhit: bold, fearless

Nabhya: central; another name for Shiva

Nabodh: one who has arisen from the sky, a cloud

Nadal: belonging to a river; fortunate

Nagaj: born from a mountain

Nahush: fellowman; another name for Vishnu and Krishna

Naimish: for a short while; a pilgrimage spot

Nainar: one who observes; a writer

Naishadh: king of Nishadhas; another name for Nala

Nakesh: lord of the sky; another name for Indra

Nakuja: born of an anthill; another name for Valmiki

Nakul: a son; a musical instrument; the fourth Pandav known for his beauty; another name for Shiva

Nalesh: king of flowers

Nalik: arrow; spear; lotus, flower

Nalin: the lotus, water lily; water

Naman: name, famous

Namat: bending, bowing

Namesh: lord of offering, one who is worshipped

Namit: bowed; a devotee; humble

Nandant: happiness; a son; friend; ruler

Nandik: one who gives pleasure; one of Shiva's attendants; a pupil of Gautama Buddha

Nandin: son; happy; Shiva's bull, the chief attendant of Shiva; another name for Shiva

Naran: that which belongs to men, that which is human

Narant: destroyer of men

Narman: joke, humour, jest

Narun: leader of men

Nathan: protector, controller; another name for Krishna

Navaj: new born, new moon

Naval: new

Navan: to appreciate

Navisth: new; youngest

Nayat: one who leads

Nihal: happy, satisfied

Nikash: horizon

Nikunj: an abode; secretive, mysterious

Nilaj: produced in the blue mountain; blue steel

Nilaksh: blue-eyed

Nilay: a place of refuge

Nilibh: with a blue colour; moon; cloud; bee

Nimal: clean, pure, bright

Nimay: adjusted; a sage

Nimesh: moment; eye wink; a son of Garuda

Nimey: to be measured; one whose character is known

Nimish: twinkling of an eye; a son of Garuda, another name for Vishnu

Nimit: permanent; erected

Ninad: gentle murmur, humming, sound

Nipak: intelligent, wise

Nirad: cloud

Nirat: engrossed, absorbed; happy, contented

Nirjit: won, conquered

Nirmit: created, built

Nirvrit: happy, peaceful, contented

Nishith: born of night

Nisidh: gift, offering

Nistul: unequalled

Nistush: pure

Nitarun: the first light of dawn

Nityayaj: never distracted

Nivan: reigned, tied

Nivid: instructions, invocation

Ogan: wave; assembled; united

Ohas: mode of conveyance; appreciation; thought

Ojal: grand; vision

Ojas: energy; grandeur; power; water; a son of Krishna

Ojasin: mighty, strong

Ojaski: courageous; shining

Ojasya: possessing virility, mighty, strong

Ojayit: on whom courage has been bestowed; brave

Ojisth: best among powerful, strong; a sage

Okithak: an orator, preacher; a brahmin who studies the prayers of *Sama Veda*

Oman: life-giving; safety; favour; friend

Opash: support, pillar

Paajas: energy; strength; shine, brightness, heaven and earth

Padvaya: a leader, guide

Palaksh: white

Panav: a small drum, a cymbal; a prince

Panik: the hand

Panisth: very beautiful

Panit: one who is appreciated

Paniya: one who is praised

Parag: the pollen of a flower; aromatic; illustrious

Paraj: gold

Paran: leaf; feather; full of leaves

Parayush: reaching the highest age; another name for Brahma

Parigh: a line of clouds crossing the sun at sunrise or sunset

Parijit: famous, illustrious

Parijval: enveloped by flames, to burn brightly

Pariman: abundant; plenty

Pariprit: one who is full of love and affection

Paritosh: happy

Parmand: intelligent; pure

Paroksh: one which cannot be observed; ambigious; a king of the lunar race

Parshav: the rib region, side; heaven and earth; an ancient Buddhist teacher

Parth: son of Pritha; son of the earth; prince, king; name for Arjuna; a king of Kashmir

Parthiv: belonging to the earth; grand; earthen; prince; king; warrior

Parvatiya: belonging to the mountains; a king mentioned in the *Mahabharata*

Parvit: enveloped, covered; the bow of Brahma

Paryank: bed; a specific posture of sitting; a mountain regarded as son of Vindhya

Paryetr: conqueror

Pashak: an ornament of the feet

Patav: clever; sharp

Pathas: a particular spot; water; air

Pauinah: size; another name for Shiva

Pavak: pure, clean; clear; glitter

Pavayitr: one who purifies

Payas: milk, water, rain

Payodhi: the limits, boundary; the ocean; the halo around the sun and moon; the circumference of a circle

Pehlaj: first born

Pradhi: the disc of the moon

Pradyut: lit, shining

Pragahi: knowledgeable

Pragit: one that is well-sung

Pragitya: famous, illustrious

Pragr: mountain peak

Pragun: one which is full of good qualities; straightforward, honest

Prahas: laughter; a display of colours; another name for Shiva

Praj: offspring; man

Prajanin: efficent

Prajas: born, produced

Prajin: efficent, wind, air

Prajit: conquering

Prajivin: bubbling with life, active, energetic

Prajval: lighted, inflamed

Praketa: understanding, knowledge

Prakrit: natural

Pramat: intelligent, prudent

Pranank: a living being, one who gives life

Pranav: the syllable *Om*

Pranaya: one who leads

Pranit: fire consecrated by prayer; nice, pleasing

Pranjal: honest, straight-forward

Pranshu: tall; strong

Pranut: famous; appreciated

Prashrit: humble, well-behaved; extensive

Pratik: mein; symbol; a part

Pratinav: new, young

Pratip: opposite; grandfather of Bhishma

Pratir: sea-shore, a river bank

Pratit: famous; knowledge, wise

Pratithi: born on an auspicious day; a sage

Pratush: happiness

Pratyush: every morning, early morning

Pravaha: to take along

Pravan: to conquer

Pravek: eminent, chief

Pravir: above all heros, prince, chief

Prayag: a spot for sacrifice; meeting place; the meeting point of 3 holy rivers Ganga, Jamuna, Sarasvati

Prayas: happiness, delight

Prayuj: objective, impetus

Prayut: amalgmation

Prinit: happy, gratified

Prithaj: son of Pritha, another name for Arjuna

Purohit: one who does *yagna, pandit*

Puspam: with eyes as beautiful as the topaz; a flower, blossom

Rafat: ascending

Rajit: bright, illuminated, brilliant

Ramak: sporting; lover; joyful; a mountain conquered by Sahadev

Rangit: one which is well coloured; good-looking

Rashmin: one who bears the rays, another name for the sun and the moon

Ratharvi: one who moves like a chariot, a naga mentioned in *Atharva Veda*

Rathasth: one who is on the chariot, one of the seven tributaries of Ganga

Rathik: one who rides a chariot

Rathin: lord of the chariot

Ratik: happy, delightful, loved

Ratnam: jewel

Ratrij: born in the night, a star

Ratujit: one who conquers the truth

Ravij: born of the sun; another name for Kama, Yama and the planet Saturn

Ravisth: one who is liked by the sun; another name for the orange tree

Rayan: always moving; a brother of Yashoda

Rayisth: very efficient; another name for Agni, Kuber, Brahma

Razak: devotee

Renesh: lord of love, another name for Kama

Ribhav: talented; a very sharp ray of the sun

Ribhvan: adroit, talented, wise

Rijul: simple, honest

Rijut: simple, honest

Rikuan: one who is jubliant with praise

Ritajit: acquiring truth

Ritam: truth-like; the divine truth; permanent; duty; a son of Dharma

Ritap: one who guards the divine truth

Ritav: belonging to a season

Ritvik: present

Rityu: truthful; a king of the lunar dynasty; a sage who was Varuna's priest

Rizvan: practice

Rohak: ascending

Rohan: rising; tree

Rohil: risen

Rohin: ascending; banyan tree, sandalwood tree; another name for Vishnu

Romik: salt; magnet

Rtish: lord of Rati, another name for Kama

Rudhir: red, blood; the planet Mars

Rudit: crying

Rudraj: made from Rudra; quicksilver, mercury

Rukmin: wearing gold ornaments; the eldest son of King Bhishma of Vidarbha

Rupam: beauty; shape

Rupesh: lord of form

Rupin: one who possesses a beautiful form

Rushat: brilliant, shining, white, bright

Rutv: speech; intensity

S

Sabhya: refined, cultured, of noble parentage
Sachint: thoughtful
Sachisth: mighty, strong, helpful
Sachit: one who leads a pure life
Sachit: wise
Sadhin: one who accomplishes; performer
Sadyant: from beginning to end, whole
Sahaj: simple; hereditary; natural; original
Sahaman: victorious

Sahanja: which can be easily won; a king

Sahanya: a huge mountain

Sahar: holy, good, a saint

Saharsh: happy, gay

Sahasya: powerful, courageous; the month of *Pausa*

Sahat: brave, strong

Sahavan: one who is courageous

Sahaya: friend, helper; another name for Shiva

Sahir: mountains

Sahisth: courageous, mighty

Sahonan: superior, brave, powerful

Sahvan: powerful, strong

Sakraj: son of Indra

Sakrajit: one who conquered Indra, another name for Meghnad

Saksham: able

Salay: friend, helper; another name for Shiva

Salil: water, flowing

Salin: one who has a house; worth appreciating

Samadar: respectable

Samaj: forest, numerous, another name for Indra

Samak: peacemaker

Samalya: adorned with garlands and crown

Saman: peaceful, pacifying; destroyer of sins; a song of praise

Samant: a chief, leader; bordering

Samantra: chanting of sacred verses

Samanyu: full of wrath; another name of Shiva

Samar: meeting point

Samarth: capable

Samedh: full of strength

Samesh: lord of equality; like the gods

Samik: calm, tranquil

Samin: peaceful, calm; consoling

Samitir: peaceful, calm

Samprit: contended, happy

Sanaj: old

Sanat: immortal; another name for Brahma

Sani: talented

Sanisth: one who profits the most

Sanjit: victorious

Saras: arising from a lake; the moon; the Indian crane; a son of Garuda

Satyak: a son of Manu

Sauman: flower

Sauram: the Vedic Mantra for Surya

Sayug: united; friend

Seerat: nature

Shakin: helpful; powerful

Shakr: mighty, strong, powerful; the number fourteen; another name for Indra

Shakunt: bird; son of Visvamitra

Shamen: delighted; prosperous; safe

Shanak: one who walks slowly

Sharan: safety, protecting, guarding

Sharanya: one who has a house; helpful; another name for Shiva

Shardhya: bold, strong

Shashank: moon

Shashvat: eternal, perennial

Shasman: appreciation; invocation

Shatik: brave, courageous

Shaurya: bravery

Shavas: strong, powerful, mighty

Shirin: the Kusa grass

Shivam: of Shiva; propitious; graceful; prosperous

Shranth: tying, binding; another name for Vishnu

Shresth: the best, chief, prominent; another name for Vishnu and Kubera

Shrutya: to be famous, illustrious

Shuant: calm, peaceful

Shubhan: shining, resplendent

Simant: the limit, boundary

Smayan: smile, mild laughter

Somal: soft, subtle

Suaksh: one with good eyes

Sudhan: principles

Sudhit: kind, generous

Sudhiv: one which shines brightly

Suham: measuring happiness

Sukrit: a holy deed; one who does good, generous; lucky; well-made

Sumahu: glorious

Sumalya: one who wears a nice garland

Sumant: easily known

Sumat: one who has a good nature; very intelligent; generous

Sumaya: one who has good plans; intelligent; a king of demons

Sutam: best among the virtuous

Sutir: a hero

Suvah: enduring

Suvan: the sun, fire, moon

Suyam: one which can be easily controlled

Svadhit: one which cannot be moved

T

Tahir: holy

Talan: musician

Talank: one with an auspicious sign; another name for Balaram and Shiva

Talin: a name for Shiva; engrossed

Tanak: a reward

Tanas: a child

Tanay: belonging to one's family; a son

Tanish: mighty, brave; active; the ocean; heaven; gold

Tanmay: comprising

Tanvir: enlightened

Tarak: freeing, saving; belonging to the stars; a minister of king Bhadraseva of Kashmir and a great devotee of Shiva

Tarakit: spread with stars

Tarang: one who moves across; waves

Tarant: the ocean

Tareya: son of Tara, another name for Angad

Tarish: raft, boat; an expert; the ocean

Tarit: one who has crossed over

Tarkash: star-eyed; a king of Nisdhas; a mountain

Tarush: conqueror

Tautik: the pearl oyester

Tavasya: strength

Tavur: the zodiac sign of Tauras

Tayin: protector

Tejal: one who brings light

Tejisth: astute; hot, burning

Tevan: sport

Tijit: the moon

Tisya: auspicious; lucky; a celestial archer; the month of *Paush*

Tryaksh: three eyed, a demon; another name for Shiva

Tueshin: ardent; boisterous

Tumit: peaceful, calm, quiet

Turanya: to be quick; a horse of the moon

Tushar: snow, mist, cold

Tushit: satisfied

Tushya: satisfied; another name for Shiva

Tuyam: powerful, strong, swift

Uchak: to look boldly; a king of the solar dynasty

Uchal: ascending the mind

Uchath: poem; appreciation

Uchit: happy, delightful; apt

Udaar: grand; lofty; generous, noble; famous

Udaarak: a nobleman; a minister of Mahisasur

Udachit: brought up, worshipped

Udaj: born in water, lotus

Udant: good; the end; news; folktale

Udarsh: brimming

Udatta: lofty, exalted, famous; present; dear; ornament; mild

Uday: rising; prosperity; achieving; grandeur; the sunrise; appearing

Udayant: ascending; end of sunrise

Udayin: ascending; prosperous; another name for Vishnu

Uddip: burning; lighting up

Uddipak: burning

Uddish: lord of divine beings; another name for Shiva

Udgam: the rising of the star; the height of a mountain

Udgat: something which has risen; a leader; observer; one of the seven chief priests of the Vedas

Udisht: ascended

Udit: ascended; produced; appearance; the sunrise

Udojas: very strong

Udrak: belonging to the water

Udrek: an idea; superiority

Udvansh: of a noble lineage

Udyat: ascending; a star

Udyot: bright, shine, sheen

Ugam: going upwards

Ugrak: strong, courageous; a serpent

Ujaas: the light before sunrise

Unmaj: coming forth

Unnat: exalted, lofty

Upanaya: leader

Ushenya: desired, longed for

Ushman: heat, warmth

Ushnish: headgear, crown

Usik: one who worships the dawn, an early riser

Utsaha: joyous; courage; patience; active

Uttank: a high cloud, a kind of cloud

Uttansh: an ornament, chaplet

Vaasav: coming from or related to the Vasus; a son of King Vasu; another name for Indra

Vadhish: one who resolves disputes; wise, seer, sage

Vagish: lord of speech, good command over language; another name for Brihaspati and Brahma

Vahati: companion; wind; a river

Vahin: one who bears, Shiva as the bearer of the world

Vaidat: one who knows

Vaidhav: son of the moon; another name for Mercury

Vaidhrit: lying on the same side; a specific position of the sun and the moon.

Vaidyut: appearing from lightning, brilliant

Vainavik: a flute player

Vairag: one who is above material things

Vairat: a precious stone; an earthworm; a son of Dhritarashtra

Vaistra: the world

Vaitalin: a magician,

Vajin: efficient; heroic, warlike; manly; the number seven

Vakman: speech; hymn of praise

Vakmya: praiseworthy

Vaktr: speaker; wise;

Vanas: wish, desire

Vanisth: generous

Vardhan: growing; bestower of prosperity; a son of Krishna and Mitravinda; another name for Shiva

Vardhin: increasing

Vardhit: increasing; strong; happy

Variman: the best

Varin: one who possesses a lot of gifts

Varish: lord of waters, ocean, another name for Varuna

Varisth: best; eminent; leader

Varshman: body; auspicious; good-looking; grand

Vartin: one who observes vows; worshipping

Varuth: safety; house; an Anga king

Vasesh: giver of boons

Vasujit: conqueror of wealth

Vatesh: lord of the banyan tree

Vayya: a friend; a demon

Vedashu: a famous carrier; a river

Vedesh: lord of *Vedas*

Vedhas: pious, holy; courgeous; one who creates

Vedin: emotional; another name for Brahma

Vedish: lord of the wise; another name for Brahma

Veduk: one who wishes to gain knowledge

Vehaan: morning, dawn

Vibhas: brought; illuminated; a deity; a *raag*; one of the seven suns

Vibhav: a companion; another name for Shiva

Vidur: knowledgeable; wise, talented

Vidyesh: lord of learning, another name for Shiva

Vidyot: shining, bright

Vihag: airborne, an arrow, bird; another name for the sun and moon.

Vipul: huge, bountiful.

Viraj: one who rules far and wide; king; eminent

Viral: rare

Virat: grand, magnificient

Virav: echoing; the horse of sage Agastya

Vishrut: famous, illustrious; joyous; a son of Vasudeva

Vitarag: one who is above worldly pleasures; calm

Vrayas: with superior powers

Wabar: truth
Wabh: wisdom, prudence; grandeur
Wadid: lover, companion
Wafiq: friend
Wahab: large-hearted
Wahat: noise, sound; strong; prince
Waheed: good-looking
Wahij: blaze, fire
Wajih: thick, strong

Wamiq: lover, beloved
Waqar: humble, gentle
Wasam: beautiful, good-looking
Wasan: idol
Wusul: arrival; accomplishment; strength

Yadish: lord of marine animals

Yahav: swift, active

Yajak: worshipper; liberal

Yajat: pious; divine; respectable; worthy of worship; admirable; another name for Shiva

Yajnesh: lord of the sacrificial fire; another name for Vishnu and the sun

Yaman: patient; governing

Yati: ascetic, devotee

Yatin: ascetic, devotee

Yatnuk: making efforts

Yavisth: youngest, last born

Yayashva: famous, known

Yayati: wanderer

Zachariah: God's rememberance

Zadeer: novel

Zafar: accomplishment

Zahan: eminent, intelligent

Zahid: wise

Zaki: saintly

Zakir: one with a sharp memory

Zamir: courageous; good-looking

Zanan: clever, talented; brave
Zanib: follower
Zaniq: firm, steady
Zarab: white; honey
Zaraq: blue-eyed
Zareen: golden
Zarn: good light
Zayan: long-lasting, patient, strong
Zia: enlightened
Zishan: respectable
Zuber: clean

Abhidha: name

Abhigya: expert; intelligent

Abhikhya: radiant; fame

Abhivibha: enlightening

Adrija: daughter of the mountains; goddess Parvati

Adrika: a small mountain; name of an apsara

Adya: first; unequalled; the earth

Ahana: immortal, one who cannot be killed; a person who is born during the day

Ahwana: bidding, call

Ahwanita: desired, invited, guest

Aishwarya: prosperity

Aksayini: not dying

Ambhini: born of water

Aminya: pure, clean, untouched

Amirah: full; rich; grand; ruler, princess

Amiya: nectar; compassionate, gentle

Amrisha: real

Amshula: bright, radiant

Anabhra: cloudless; clarity of thought

Anadhika: without a superior

Anadya: without a beginning, immortal, divine; name of an apsara

Anala: made of fire; without any blemish; one of the daughters of Daksh; wife of Kashyap; mother of trees and creepers

Anamra: twisted; favourable

Ananta: without an end, immortal; divine; the earth; another name for Parvati

Anantika: simple

Anantya: small

Ananya: unequalled

Anasuya: without hatred; one of the daughters of Kardama and Devahuti; wife of sage Atri

Anata: straight; a daughter of Atri and Anasuya and the mother of fruits

Anindya: beyond condemnation

Anitya: momentary

Ansruta: not heard of; unique

Antika: elder sister

Anubha: lightning

Anubhavya: learnt through experience; divine truth

Anula: tamed, gentle, agreeable; a female Arhat or Buddhist saint

Anunita: prayer, affability

Anupa: without an equal, unique; a pond, bank of a river; a sage

Anurima: fond, attached

Anvita: following after

Anya: boundless

Aranyani: wilderness, desert, forest, the goddess of wilderness

Arhana: worship, honoured; adored

Arikta: full, ample; contented

Artika: elder sister

Arundhati: loyalty

Aruni: gold, ruby; glowing red; red cow; dawn; treasured; enlightening; ardent; sacred; Aruna as a female in Indra's assembly

Ashivuka: little mare

Atiriya: beloved; adored; pursued; rare

Avisya: desire; warmth

Ayati: a descendant; grandeur; heirs

Azizah: beloved; rare, precious

Badarayani: novel; young; clean; perfume

Bagesri: prosperity

Bahair: beautiful, delicate woman

Bahar: spring; orange, rose; glory; elegance, beauty

Bahulika: many times, multiplied; multifaceted personality; the Pleiades

Bakuli: lady of the blossoms; nature; a *ragini* of *Bhairava*

Bakulika: a flower of the bakula tree

Bakulita: adorned with bakula blossoms

Balada: giver of strength; a daughter of Raudrasva

Balini: mighty, strong; the constellation of *Asvini*

Barhayita: as beautiful as the eye on a peacock feather

Barhina: decorated with peacock feathers

Benazir: unequalled, matchless, without comparison, peerless

Beniyaz: without any wants; without any worries; another name for God

Bhairavi: dreadful; consort of Bhairav, a terrifying form of Kali, a *raag*, one of the forms of Durga

Bhamini: shining, radiant; beautiful, glorious; the wife of King Aviksit of Vaishali

Bhanavi: descendant of the sun, as brilliant as the sun; sacred; shining; a river crossed by Rama and Lakshman; another name for Yamuna river

Bhavanika: resident of a castle

Bhaviki: real; pure, natural; compassionate

Bhavila: worthy; good

Bhavini: encouraging; emotions; virtuous; pretty; famous; affectionate; sensitive

Bhavya: grand; existing; apt; pretty; honest, pious; a son of Priyavrata

Bhomira: born of the earth; the coral; productive; patient

Bhraji: shine, glory, fame

Bhumi: earth, soil; an object of existence; earth as a goddess who was the daughter of Brahma and wife of Mahavishnu

Bhuva: fire; the earth

Chaitali: intelligent; belonging to the mind

Chaitri: born during the spring time; as beautiful, soft and fresh as a new blossom; always happy

Chakrika: a name for Lakshmi

Chaksani: pleasing to the eyes; illuminating

Chanchala: changeable, always moving; lightning; a river; another name for Lakshmi

Chandrakriti: shaped as a moon, as beautiful as the moon

Chandrika: moonlight; fair; calm, cool, soothing; fenugreek; cardarmom

Charchika: repeating a word; fragrant; inviting; a tutelary goddess; another name for Durga

Charuvi: grand; another name for Kubera's wife Bhadra

Chavi: an image, reflection; beauty; grandeur; a ray of light

Chetaki: capable of perceiving or feeling things; spanish jasmine; black myrobalan

Chitrali: a wonderful lady; a friend

Chitrani: another name for river Ganga

Chitrarathi: one with a bright chariot; a form of Durga

Chitrashri: one bestowed with divine beauty

Chitrini: one who possesses various talents; brightly ornamented; possesses marks of excellence

Chitrita: adorned with ornaments; painted

Dakshayani: coming from Daksha; gold or an ornament made of gold; daughter of a perfect being, daughter of Daksha; another name for goddess Durga

Darpanika: a small looking glass

Darshani: worth seeing; another name for goddess Durga

Dasergi: daughter of a fisherman; another name for Satyarati

Dayadi: one who inherits; daughter; heiress

Dayita: compassionate; beloved, cherished, dear

Devashree: divine goddess; another name for Lakshmi

Devesmita: with a divine smile; heroine of *Katha Saritsagara*

Devika: minor goddess; god-like; a class of goddess of an inferior order

Dhamini: religious, pious; a type of perfume

Dhanvanya: treasure of the jungle; an oasis

Dharini: possessing something; a mystical verse to be used; assuage pain; a daughter of Svadha; the wife of Agnimitra; the earth personified as wife of Dhruva

Dhishana: knowledge, wisdom, grace; goddesses, the goddess of abundance; the wife of Havirdhana, daughter of Agni

Dhita: born of a bird, a daughter

Dhiti: thought, wisdom, reflection, prayer

Dhriti: fixed; order; constant; happiness; personified as the daughter of Daksha; wife of Dharma; a goddess; one of the sixteen digits of the moon; the wife of Rudra Manu

Dhyeya: ideal; aim

Didhi: fixed; stable; shining

Didhiti: fixed, stable; devotion; inspiration

Didvi: bright, shining; risen as a star; another name for Brihaspati

Diksha: initiation into a religious order; the initiation; personified as the wife of Soma, Rudra, Ugra and Rudra Vamadeva.

Dipaksit: bright-eyed

Dipana: bright; passion; that which kindles in flames; an attendant of Devi

Dipra: shining, bright

Dirghika: a tall girl; an oblong lake; a daughter of Visvakarman

Divija: born of the sky, born of heaven; divine, a god

Divolka: fallen from the sky, a meteor

Drshika: pretty, beautiful

Druti: softened; the wife of Naksa and mother of Gaya

Dyotana: shining, bright

- **Dyuthi:** shining, bright

Ekaja: only child

Ekakini: solitary, alone

Ekangika: made of sandalwood; fair; often; auspicious; loved by the gods

Ekanta: beautiful; devoted to one

Ekantika: devoted to one objective

Ekaparna: single-leafed, living on a single leaf; the daughter of Himavana and Mena; the sister of Durga, Aparna and Ekapatala and the wife of sage Devata

Ekisa: one goddess, the primal goddess

Eksika: eye

Ekyastika: a single string of pearls

Ena: doe, spotted, a black antelope; another name for the zodiac sign of Capricorn

Enaksi: doe-eyed

Esha: objective, wish, desire

Eshanika: fulfilling wishes; a goldsmith's balance

Eshita: wanted, longing

Esikha: one that achieved the objective; an arrow, a dart

Eti: arrival

F

Faiha: expanse; fragrant, aromatic

Faihah: perfume, fragrance

Fainan: one with beautiful, luscious hair

Fanhanah: a female artist

Faqihah: a woman well-versed in law and divinity, theologian, school mistress

Farah: joy, happiness, gay

Faranah: one who is famous, glorious; Faridun's mother

Faridah: solitary; different; large pearl

Farihan: happy; woman

Farya: friend

Farzi: queen at chess

Farzin: intelligent; wise; queen at chess

Fasah: break forth and shine in full splendour

Fasanah: a tale, fable; famous

Fatat: a young girl

Fazanah: intelligent

Firzan: queen in chess

Fisa: peacock

Frashmi: prosperity; giving; epithet of Haoma

Frayashti: worship, praise

Freya: dear

Freyana: dear

Frohar: an angel; a sublime spirit which protects the soul as a guardian angel

Gandhalika: aromatic; an apsara; another name for goddess Parvati and Satyavati; the mother of Vyasa

Gandharvi: the speech of a gandharv; the granddaughter of sage Kashyap and Krodhvasha; the daughter of Surabhi and the mother of horses; another name for Durga; a seductive water nymph who haunts the banks of rivers

Gandhini: aromatic; another name for Prithvi

Gangika: like the river Ganga; one who is as holy, pure as the Ganga river

Gathika: a song

Gaunika: valuable; the jasmine flower

Gaurika: like Gauri, fair, pretty

Gayanti: belonging to Gaya; wife of king Gaya, the royal sage

Gayantika: singing; a Himalayan cave

Geshna: a singer

Ghazal: a lyric poem; words of love sonnet, love poetry

Gira: speech; voice; vocabulary; song; a Vedic hymn; another name for Sarasvati

Girika: the peak of a mountain; the daughter of river Saktimati

Girikarni: a lotus

Girisa: lady of the mountains, another name for Parvati

Gitali: lover of song

Gopika: one who looks after the herd; another name for Radha

Gulfroz: as beautiful as a flower

Gunjika: humming; images; meditation; the rosary pea

Gurnika: wife of a teacher; a companion of Devayani

Haima: of the snow; golden; another name for Parvati and Ganga

Hamra: the colour red; fair woman

Hansika: swan; a daughter of Surabhi who is said to support the southern region

Hansini: swan, goose

Hanum: a lady, woman

Hardika: sincere

Haridra: turmeric

Harikina: completely concentrated on Vishnu

Harinaksi: doe-eyed

Harini: doe; greenery; yellow jasmine; a golden image; an apsara

Haritalika: bringer of greenery; goddess of fertility; fourth day of the bright half of the month of *Bhadra* personified as a goddess of pleasure

Hariti: yellowish-brown colour, green; fresh; the goddess of Rajgriha

Harmya: house, palace, mansion

Harshala: happy

Harshita: full of happiness

Harshvina: a lute that delights

Hasika: blooming, smiling, spreading happiness

Hasnat: beautiful, fair

Hastha: a star

Hemangi: a girl with golden body

Hemangini: girl with golden body

Himaja: daughter of the snow, daughter of the Himavana, another name for Parvati

Himalini: completely covered with snow

Himani: glacier, snow, avalanche; another name for Parvati

Hiranya: golden

Hityshi: well-wisher

Hityshini: well-wisher

Hiya: heart

I

Iaikhyata: unity

Iaiktya: unity

Iaishwaya: wealth

Ida: a moment; wisdom; the earth as a giver of food; the daughter of Vayu, who was the wife of Dhruv and mother of Utkal

Idika: belonging to Ida; another name for Prithvi or the earth

Iditri: one who appreciates

Iha: longing, wish

Ihita: wished for

Ijya: an image; a gift; charity; worship

Iksha: right

Ikshenya: worth-looking

Ikshita: visible, seen

Ikslada: that which renders sweetness, sweet-tongued

Ilakshi: eye of the earth, the axis of the earth, centre of the earth

Ilesha: queen of the earth

Ilhana: music, sweet voice

Ilika: small; earth, a minor form of the earth

Ilina: very intelligent, a daughter of Medhatithi; Yama's daughter

Ilrika: protector of the earth; the five stars at the head of the constellation Orion

Impana: sweet-voiced

Inakshi: sharp-eyed

Indrakshi: one who has eyes like Indra, a goddess

Indrani: consort of Indra

Indrayani: wife of Indra

Inika: small earth

Ipsa: longing, wish

Ipsita: wished for, longed for

Iraja: daughter of the wind

Isha: power

Ishana: supreme, another name for Durga

Ishani: ruling; the wood from sami tree which when rubbed produces fire; another name for Durga

Ishanika: belonging to the north-east

Ishika: a painter's brush; the pen used for writing auspicious things

Ishta: that which is worshipped through sacrifice; the sami tree

Jagavi: born of the world

Jagti: belonging to the universe, heaven and hell together, another name for the earth

Jahnavi: born from the ear; the daughter of Jahnu, another name for river Ganga

Jalavalika: surrounded by water, lightning

Jallata: a stream of water, a wave

Janhita: one who thinks about the welfare of mankind

Jarita: old, rotten, a sarngika bird who had four sons by sage Mandapala

Javitri: spice, mace

Javlitri: bright, resplendent, shining

Jaya: victory, victorious

Jayana: giver of victory; armour; a daughter of Indra

Jayani: one who brings victory; a daughter of Indra

Jayanti: one who is victorious in the end; a flag; a daughter of Indra and the wife of Sukra

Jayita: victorious

Jayitri: victorious

Jitya: victorious

Jivantika: giver of long life

Jivika: the source of life, water; occupation

Joshika: cluster of birds; a young woman

Joshya: happy

Jugisha: one who wishes to be victorious

Jvalita: burning, bright

Kadambari: belonging to Kadamba tree; female cuckoo; wine obtained from the Kadamba tree; another name for Sarasvati

Kahala: impish, naughty; a young woman; a kind of musical instrument; an apsara; Varuna's wife

Kahini: impish, naughty; young

Kairavi: moonlight

Kakalika: with a low and sweet voice; an apsara

Kalandika: one who grants art or skills; wisdom

Kalpani: as blue as the peacock's tail; night-time

Kamayaka: desired abode; the forest in which the Pandavas hid during their exile

Kamayani: the mirror of love

Kamita: longed for, wished for

Kamra: longed for, pretty, affectionate

Kamuka: longed for, the madhavi creeper

Kamya: pretty, desirable, hard-working; a celestial woman

Kana: girl, an eye

Kanaka: born of sand; another name for Sita

Kanavi: small kite

Kanika: an atom, very small

Kanina: young; the pupil of the eye; a boy

Kanistha: the youngest

Kanita: iris of the eye

Kanka: scent of the lotus; a daughter of Ugrasena and sister of Kanka

Kanksha: desire, wish, inclination

Kankshini: one who wishes

Kanyala: a girl

Kanyana: girl

Karalika: sword; another name for Durga

Karmishta: extremely hard-working

Karnika: creeper; heart of lotus; earring,

Kashvi: shining, beautiful

Kastha: peak; important point; appearance; water, the sun; a daughter of Daksha; the wife of Kashyap

Katyayani: attired in red; another name for Parvati

Kaushalika: gift, an offering

Kavika: poetess

Kenati: above all; another name for Rati, the wife of Kama

Krinjala: brook

Kriti: creation

Kritvi: accomplished

Kritya: action; accomplishment; proper; a female deity; a river

Kshamya: the earth

Kshema: safety, security; welfare; peace; another name for Durga

Kshiti: house, home, earth, soil of the earth
Kshitija: born of the earth; another name for Sita
Kunjika: belonging to the bower
Kusamita: adorned with flowers, made of flowers

Lakshaki: made of or dyed with lac; another name for Sita.

Lakshita: visible, seen; another name for Sita

Lalantika: a long necklace

Lalatika: a piece of jewellery worn on the forehead

Lalitaka: favourite daughter; an ancient pilgrimage of Brahma

Lalitangi: one with a beautiful body

Lalitasya: affectionate, charming, elegant

Lavalika: a small vine

Lavalina: concentrated; devoted

Lavana: pretty

Lavangi: belonging to the clove plant; an apsara

Lavanya: pretty, beautiful

Lepakshi: with painted eyes

Lipika: the written word, alphabet; anointing

Lohitika: the gem ruby

Lohitya: rice; the *Puranic* name for river Brahmaputra

Lokanya: one who is worthy of heaven

Madayanti: exciting; arabian jasmine; another name for Durga

Madayantika: exciting; arabian jasmine

Madhavi: sweet; an intoxicating drink; honey; sacred basil; the daughter of king Yayati; another name for Durga and Subhadra

Madhavika: one who collects honey; a creeper

Madira: nectar, wine; another name for Durga; another name for the wife of Varuna and the goddess of wine

Maghya: born in the month of *Magha*; the blossom of jasmine

Mahelika: a woman

Mahika: dew, frost

Mahima: grandeur, power

Mahita: flowing on the earth; river; greatness,

Mahiya: joyful, delight

Makshika: bee

Malashika: garlanded; a *ragini*

Malatika: made of jasmine

Malavi: princess of the Malavas, the wife of king Asvapati of Madra; a *ragini*

Malavika: belonging to Malva; the heroine of a drama by Kalidasa

Mallika: jasmine; daughter; necklace; intoxicating drink; queen

Manani: wife of Manu

Mananya: one who is worthy of appreciation

Manasvi: one who controls the mind; wise

Manasvini: one who controls the mind; virtuous; another name for Durga

Manavika: a young girl

Manayi: Manu's wife

Mandira: belonging to the temple; pious, holy; a slow sound; metallic cymbals producing a musical sound

Manika: jewellery; a particular weight

Maninga: treasure of jewels; a river

Manini: determined; self-respecting; an apsara

Manishi: longed by the heart

Manishika: comprehended; wisdom

Maniya: glass bead

Manorita: belonging to the mind; longing

Mantika: contemplative; an *Upanishad*

Mantrana: advice

Manushi: woman; soft-hearted

Manya: one who deserves respect

Manyanti: respectable

Marali: female swan

Maralika: small swan

Marichika: mirage, illusion

Marya: the limit

Matali: mother's friend; an attendant of Durga

Matallika: anything excellent of its kind

Mayuranki: with peacock marks; a jewel

Mayurika: with peacock feathers; a *ragini*

Medhani: wise; the consort of Brahma

Medhya: fresh, clean; holy, wise, intelligent

Mekhala: belt; the slope of a mountain; another name for river Narmada

Menaja: a name for Parvati

Menita: intelligent

Midhushi: abundant

Mihika: mist, fog, snow

Minali: a fisherwoman; another name for Satyavati

Minati: fish-like; voluptuous

Mitali: friendship

Mitusi: one who has limited needs

Mrgisna: doe-eyed

Mridvika: soft, gentle; mild

Mrigekshana: deer-eyed

Mrinali: lotus stalk

Mrinalika: a lotus root

Mrinalini: a lotus; aromatic; holy, dear to the gods

Mringangi: soft-bodied, delicate

Mritsa: earth, aromatic soil

Mritsna: earth, very fertile soil

Mrkshini: a rain cloud

Mrtfika: earth

Muralika: a small flute

Naazima: song

Nabhanya: arising from the heaven, heavenly

Nainika: pupil of the eye

Nalakini: a multitude of lotuses; a lake

Namita: bowed, bent down, meek

Namya: to be bowed; the night

Nanantika: destroying; a river of ancient India

Nandika: one who gives pleasure; Indra's pleasure ground

Nandini: happy; daughter; another name for Durga

Naristha: dear to woman; the arabian jasmine

Navangi: a beautiful woman

Navika: novel, young, fresh

Navina: young

Navisthi: songs of appreciation; a hymn

Naviya: new, young

Navya: new

Nayaja: daughter of wisdom

Nayayika: logician

Nichika: divided into parts; comprising all parts; a whole

Nichita: fully covered; a holy river of ancient India, another name for Ganga

Nidhyati: meditation, reflection

Niharika: misty; the Milky Way

Nimisha: twinkling of an eye

Nirajakshi: lotus-eyed, beautiful

Nirajita: enlightened

Nirbha: to shine forth; appearance

Niriksha: not visible to the eye; anticipation
Nirmita: constructed
Nishama: unequalled
Nishika: honest, pure
Nishita: night
Nupur: an ornament worn on the toes, anklet
Nyja: natural

Odati: rejuvenating; the dawn

Ojasvini: brave; shining; energetic; powerful

Omala: giver of the Om; the holy word for the earth; giver of birth, life and death; earth

Omisha: goddess of the sacred syllable Om; goddess of birth, life and death

Ondarya: generous; broadminded

Oorja: name of a sage's wife; power

Oormi: sea wave; a term in music

Oormika: sea wave; humming of a bee
Oorna: name of sage's wife
Oorvi: the earth

Pakshini: day of the full moon; a female bird

Palakshi: white

Palashini: covered with leaves; a river

Panya: appreciated; grand; eminent

Parama: that which is beyond physical world; the perfect woman

Paridhi: halo around the sun or the moon, a lamp or halo around the head of deities

Parinistha: one who is at the top of the summit; one who has complete knowledge

Parinita: complete; a married woman

Parivita: free; liked by everyone; the bow of Brahma

Parnasha: one who feeds on leaves; a river personified by an apsara of Varuna's court

Parnini: leafy; an apsara

Parokshi: beyond understanding; ambigious

Parthivi: daughter of the earth; another name for Sita or Lakshmi

Parvini: a festival, holiday

Pastya: house; goddess of household matters

Patangika: little bird; a little bee

Pauravi: descended from Puru; a wife of Vasudeva; a wife of Yudhisthira; a *raga*

Pavaka: one who purifies; storm

Pavaki: purifying; the *Vedic* name of Sarasvati

Pavitra: pious, clean; beneficiant; sacred basil, a river

Phalaya: flowers, buds

Prachika: driving; a female falcon

Pradhi: very wise

Pragati: progress

Praharsha: happiness

Prajakta: mother of the people; goddess of creation

Prajna: intelligence; wisdom; a form of Sarasvati

Prajvala: lighted

Prakriti: natural, nature personified as the Supreme Spirit

Prakya: shining, mein; famous, celebrity

Prama: foundation

Pramika: best, greatest; one who fulfils desires

Pramiti: understanding, wisdom, prudence

Pranati: bowing; offering to God

Pranayita: alive, bubbling with life

Praniti: conduct, guidance

Pranyga: wisdom; safety, care

Prathana: prayer

Pratichya: from the west; one who is blessed with foresight

Pratika: symbolic; pretty; an image

Pratistha: stable, foundation, support

Pravara: best among women; a river of *Puranic* fame

Prerana: inspiration, direction
Prerita: one who is encouraged
Prestha: dearest; most loved
Prishavi: soft, mild, gentle
Prithika: jasmine
Puloma: one who is excited
Puravi: belonging to the east; alive; a *ragini*
Puruvi: one who fulfills wishes; a *ragini*

Radhami: worship

Radhana: speech

Ragini: melody; love; elder sister of Parvati; a form of Lakshmi; a musical mode in Indian classical music

Rakshita: guarded; an apsara who was the daughter of Kashyap and Pradha

Ramani: affectionate, happy, pleasure, joy

Ramanika: affectionate; happy, gay; beautiful

Ramayani: the mirror of Rama; one who is well-versed in the *Ramayana*

Ranhita: efficient, quick

Ranvita: happy, delightful

Ranya: pleasant

Rasana: one who knows the taste; the tongue, taste; understanding

Rashmika: a tiny ray of light

Rasika: one who is tasteful, elegant, gracious

Rasya: emotional, full of feelings

Rathya: crossroads; a group of chariots

Ratija: daughter of the truth

Ratrika: the night

Raupya: one that is made of silver, a *Puranic* river in ancient India

Rebha: one who sings praises

Reva: agile, quick; wife of Karna; another name for Narmada and Kali

Ribhya: worshipped

Riddhi: prosperity, wealth, abundance; superiority; one of wives of Ganesha; another name for Lakshmi and Parvati

Riddhima: auspicious; prosperous; the season of spring; love

Rista: sword; another name for the mother of apsaras

Riya: one who sings

Royina: ascending, growing

Rupangi: one with a beautiful body

Rupika: one who has a beautiful body, appearance; coin of gold and silver

Rushati: white, fair-complexioned

Rutika: one who ascends; wish

Saachika: truthful

Sadhaka: swift, efficient; another name for Durga

Sahima: covered with snow

Sahita: proximity; a river

Sahitra: enduring

Sama: peaceful, tranquil; equanimity; a year

Samajya: illustrious, famous

Samali: a bouquet of flowers

Samani: calm, peaceful

Samasti: accomplishing; whole; the universe

Samichi: appreciation; eulogy; a doe; an apsara

Samiha: longing, desire

Samisha: dart

Samriti: meeting

Sanah: radiant, bright, resplendent

Sananda: joyful, delightful; a form of Lakshmi

Sanitra: gift; an offering to the god

Sanjanya: merciful, generous; loving; friendly; compassionate

Saparya: worship; admiration

Sara: fixed; hard; valuable; best

Saranya: one who protects; one who gives shelter; another name for Durga

Sarvika: universal; complete, whole

Sashrika: one who is endowed with beauty, grace; fortune

Saumya: related to the moon; peaceful; a pearl; gentle; another name for Durga

Sauvarna: made of gold

Sauviri: daughter of a hero

Savini: one who gives nectar; a river

Shaini: prosperity; another name for goddess Mansa

Shakuntika: a small bird

Shamika: tranquil

Shansita: desired; appreciated; famous

Sharmistha: the lucky one; wife of Yayati

Sheralini: one who has moss-like surface; a river

Shivika: palanquin

Shreya: most beautiful; best

Shrila: granted by Lakshmi; auspicious; prosperous; joyful; famous

Shubhya: auspicious

Shuchika: pious, holy; an aspara

Sirina: night

Smera: smiling, affable; evident

Snakriti: good-looking

Snigdha: soft; affable; brilliant; charming; graceful

Somali: deer to the moon

Spandana: heartbeat; very beautiful

Srinjayi: granter of victory

Sriti: path, road

Sthira: determined; another name for the earth

Stuti: invocation

Suchita: favourable; pious

Sudiksha: another name for Lakshmi

Suhela: easily approachable

Sukala: a good part; very talented

Sukanya: a pretty girl

Sukriti: benevolent, generous; auspicious

Suloma: one with beautiful hair; Indian redwood

Sumantika: the Indian white rose

Sumaya: well-planned; a daughter of Maya

Sunaya: just; well-behaved; the mother of a Jain Tiranthankara

Sunayana: one with beautiful eyes

Suniksha: one with beautiful ornaments

Surana: happy, delightful; making a pleasing sound; a river

Surmya: good-looking

Suryani: wife of the sun

Suvali: graceful, elegant

Suvena: with a beautiful braid; *Puranic* river which sage Markandeya saw in the stomach of the child Krishna

Sveni: white

Talika: the palm; nightingale

Taluni: a young girl

Tama: night

Tamra: copper-crested

Tamrika: copperish

Tanishi: might, strength, bravery; a daughter of Indra; another name for the earth

Tanuvi: a svelte figure

Tapani: heat; a river

Taraka: star, falling star, meteor; the eye; Brihaspati's wife

Tarakini: starry; night

Tarani: a boat

Tarika: one who belongs to the stars

Tarini: one who helps to cross over; rescuing another name for Durga

Tarita: the forefinger; the leader; another name for Durga

Tarushi: victory

Tilika: a small mark of sandalwood

Timila: a musical instrument

Titiksa: patience

Trayi: wisdom, comprehension; the three *Vedas*

Trishala: the mother of Mahavira

Trishna: thirst; daughter of Kama

Triya: young woman

Tulini: the cotton tree

Turya: one who possesses power

Tushita: contented

Tvisha: bright, shining, resplendent

Tvishi: boisterous, brilliance, active, enthusiasm

Uchchata: height; excellence
Udantika: protected, contented
Udayanti: ascending; eminent; good
Udbhuti: appearing; existence
Udgiti: singing
Uditi: the sunrise
Udvaha: continuation; a daughter
Udvahni: glowing; shining
Udyati: height; ascending

Ujjesha: victorious

Ujjiti: victory

Ujjval: bright, clean

Ulkushi: a meteor

Unnati: flourishing; advance; dignity; ascending; the wife of Garuda; a daughter of Daksha and wife of Dharma

Upanayika: fit for an offering

Upasti: admiration, worship

Urjal: active, strength; food, water, breath; another name for Parvati

Urjani: belonging to energy; daughter of the sun; goddess of strength

Urmika: seawave; ringfinger; humming of bees

Urmya: path; night; *Vedic* goddess of light

Urvara: fertile soil, the earth

Urvi: the earth, heaven and earth together

Ushana: longing, desire

Ushija: born of a desire, longing; active; enthusiastic; beautiful

Utkalika: one who desires to be famous; a bud; a wave

Utkanika: wish, desire

Utkarika: composed of precious material; made of milk and ghee

Utkhala: perfume

Uttarika: crossing over; delivering; a boat; a river

Uttejini: animated, excited

Vaidehi: princess of the Videhas, another name for Sita

Vaimitra: a friend of the universe

Vainani: belonging to Venu; gold from the Venu river

Vaishalini: daughter of the great; the daughter of king Vishal

Vaishnavi: worshipper of Vishnu

Vaitarini: one who crosses the physical world; one who helps in crossing the physical world; a river which flows in Orissa

Vakshani: one who strengthens

Vallika: enveloped with vines, greenery

Vama: beautiful; a form of Durga; a queen of Kashi

Vamakshi: beautiful-eyed

Vamana: small; an apsara

Vamani: bringer of wealth; small

Vamika: situated on the left side; another name for Durga

Vanalika: belonging to the forest; sunflower

Vandya: one who is worthy of praise, admirable

Vanya: belonging to the wood; rosary pea

Varalika: goddess of power; controller of the army; another name for Durga

Varnika: of a good colour, gold

Vasvi: divine night

Vatya: storm

Vayodha: strengthening

Venika: constantly flowing; a holy river of *Puranas*

Venya: wished for

Vidipita: lighted

Viha: heaven

Vilashini: shining, bright; another name for Lakshmi

Vinayika: the consort of Ganesha

Virani: brave woman; a daughter of Brahma born from his left thumb

Virika: brave

Virya: strength, active

Vishruti: famous

Vitasta: the measure of length from the wrist to the tip of the fingers

Vyusti: first ray of dawn; beautiful; reward; happiness

Waheeda: beautiful

Wahilah: Prophet Noah's wife who was an unbeliever

Waiyah: a fine pearl

Wamika: goddess

Wamil: beautiful

Wana: turtle dove

Yahua: heaven and the earth

Yajnika: used in offering to the gods

Yakshangi: a river; alive; swift

Yamala: a river

Yamini: night

Yamya: night

Yastika: a string of pearls

Yati: patient, endurance

Yogita: attracted; wild
Yosita: woman, wife
Yubhika: numerous

Zaha: beautiful flower, blossom; radiance, shining

Zaharah: spirit; fresh; strength

Zahra: pretty, very fair; clean; calm, Prophet Mohammad's daughter

Zarenya: golden

Zarin: golden

Zeba: decorated; beautiful, graceful

Zebunisha: an ornament among women; daughter of Emperor Aurangzeb

Zeenat: fame
Zewar: jewellery
Ziba: female hyenas
Zohra: the planet Jupiter
Zulekha: beautiful
Zurlah: flower; beautiful, fair; pretty, glowing
Zusha: bracelet